Red With Memories

Rodali Kalita

/ BookLeaf
Publishing
India | USA | UK

Made with ❤ on the BookLeaf Publishing Platform
www.bookleafpub.in
www.bookleafpub.com

Dedication

To every person who touched my life, even for a moment.

Preface

These poems are pieces of my heart—of love and loss, fire and longing. They are the moments that broke me, the people who left, and the memories that color everything red. Some words whisper, some scream, some just bleed quietly—but all of them are part of the same story: a heart that dared to feel and survive.

This book is for anyone who has loved too much, lost too deeply, and still carries a fire inside.

—Rodali Kalita

Acknowledgements

This book wouldn't exist without my mother, who supported me in every word I wrote and believed in my voice even when I doubted it.

Thank you to the wounds that never fully healed, the losses, and the moments of longing, they taught me how to feel deeply and turn pain into words.

Thank you to the quiet nights, the memories that colored me red, and the fire that keeps burning, they reminded me that even in the hardest moments, there is beauty in feeling.

And most of all, thank you to the readers, who will hold these words, carry them with you, and perhaps see a part of your own story reflected in them.

—Rodali Kalita

1. Like a Moth to a Flame

If you were a cigarette,
I'd burn you down to the filter,
pulling you into me,
letting you wreck my lungs,
make me cough,
make me yours.

I'd crave the sting,
the heat searing my throat,
a rush, a poison,
a need I can't quit.
Even knowing you'd kill me,
I'd keep inhaling.

Let the smoke curl inside me,
let it settle like a death wish.
I'd die choking on you,
burning for you,
falling for you.

2. Crimson

Bleeding on the page once again,
This time with the ache of ink.

When I woke up from the stillness,
life's sharp edges found me again.
Yet in the grey, I knew a quiet.....
a peace I almost called my own.

Tragedies are like blood,
And suddenly crimson is my favourite colour.

3. The curse of 3 a.m

Blood in my lips,
Blood on my hands,
Clutching my heart, drowning in pain.
Tears ran down,
Time stood still,
And I lay in death's domain.

Everything wasn't totally fine,
Yet, fear of death, I couldn't find.
3 a.m - the most ruthless time,
As if seeking revenge on my mind.

With the pain in my heart,
It's hard to breathe every time,
I thought it was my final night.
Closed my teary eyes,
And lay still to die.

I survived!

4. Broken Hush

When my heart ripped into million pieces
Yet, I never told you
For you wouldn't care.
The weight of unspoken pain never ceases,
Hidden behind a mask, emotion threadbare.

In quiet corners of my wounded soul,
Echoes of ache,
Shredded memories,
A heart left to break.

I painted my pain with ink,
Drew stars around my scar,
Words bled onto papers,
A Symphony of brokenness
A Melody undone.

5. Ripped pages

In the quiet library of my past
Where memories align,
I found some pages stained with tears,
With edges not do fine.
Important chapters, once held dear,
I ripped them out, the hurtful parts,
Like blemishes on my brain.

These pages torn, they flutter down,
A snowstorm of regret.
Each a piece of choice, a voice, a face,
I wish to forget.
Decisions harsh, yet necessary,
A self preserving rite.
For some connections weigh us down
And dim our inner light

A tapestry of solitude, of peace.
Where once were scribbles of the past, now only grace
For though the act of ripping strings,
The aftermath is right.
Some pages must be lost, to let the remaining
ones shines bright.

6. Elegy of Beauty in Demise

The beauty of death, like a whispered sigh,
In it's stillness, we find peace.
A canvas of stars in infinite night,
A passage from darkness into eternal light.

The closing of eyes.
The end of pain.
A quiet surrender,
A comforting rest.

Death unveils a secret,
A truth we all trust.
In it's beauty, a mystery, so gentle and deep.
We embrace the unknown
Where our soul shall keep.

A journey, a passage to a tranquil peace ......

7. Masterpiece

You were the golden masterpiece
Oil smeared
Painted by the most delicate hands
With intoxicant gaze in your eyes.
A sip of allure
The most beautiful piece of art
Soft and loved
Curls twirling in soft breeze.
A beauty made in heaven.

In contrast

I was just a child's project
Crayon painted, with hues away,
Grotesque and hideous
Unloved and damaged.
Yet creative in my own ways
Cared just for your love.

It still haunts me,
how you crumpled me
and tossed me away.

Yet it's understandable

I was not *YOU!*
I was not *PERFECT!*

8. Corpse Butterfly

The butterflies are long dead,
No more wings to grace the day.
Their wings now dusty, pale and shed.
Gone are the colours, bright and fair
Just left cold whispers in the air.

All the butterflies are gone!

9. We Ended Without an Ending

(But we never started)

I felt you there, in shadows soft,
A quiet presence, never aloft,
You lingered close, but never near,
A whisper I wasn't mean to hear.

You loved me, didn't you? I think I knew,
In passing glances, the silence grew,
But I was bound to someone else's heart,
And never knew how close we would start.

I wonder now, when it's far too late,
If we were tangled by threads of fate,
If you had been bold, if I had been free,
Maybe the world would have *You* and *Me*.

But we ended without an ending, it seems,
A love that flickered in half-formed dreams,
You stayed silent, I stayed blind,
Now you're just a thought lost in time.

10. Almost. Always. Never

He walks like storms don't touch him
He doesn't speak much
but when he does
the air learn to behave.

The hills once knew our silent ride,
His shoulders strong, my nerves inside...
I sat behind the thunder
close, yet far away.

He never looked back
Didn't needed to
My body remembered
every turn,
every hum of the road
every place I almost touched
but I didn't.......

11. My Hollow Soul

Breath turns brittle, lungs retreat,
The night hums low, it's ache complete.
Why does midnight, with tender spite,
Steal my heart and dim it's light?

Each tear a thread, silent scream,
Unraveled the fabric of a distant dream.

12. The Wolves came back just to play!

In shadows deep, where secret lie
She loved him true.
With all her heart, her soul did pour
But he, a storm, her spirit tore.

He never saw her for her worth
Manipulated, dragged through the Earth
Her dreams were crushed
Her spirit strained.

Later,
 A wolf inside her heart, did wake
 Prepared to make the heaven quake
 With sharpened fangs and eyes of fire
 She planned his fall, her dark desire.

His world she shattered, piece by piece
His grip on life began to cease.
With ruthless hands and vengeful grace
She dragged him to his darkest place
No mercy found, no kindness spared.
He trembled at the force unleashed
His pleas for mercy never ceased.

But she, a wolf, just bared her teeth,
Revenge was sweet, his pain her wreath
His cries, her victory.
The Wolves came back just to play,
To hunt, to feast, to end the day.

13. Silken Passage

Life's relentless, ruthless stride,
Whispers dreams that often hide.
Yet, in the dance of shadow's waltz,
Hope persists, a fragile vault.

A kiss from Death, a soft caress.
To cradle woes in sweet regress,
Eternal slumber, a tranquil sea,
Where pain dissolves, and spirits free.

Though somber veils of endless night,
To realms where pain takes fleeting flight.
Smooth caress, a whispered balm,
In the cradle of eternal calm.

No more the echoes of life's cruel song,
A refuge sought, where hearts belong.
Forever held in the arms of peace,
Where wordly woes find sweet release.

14. Fluent in You

Your eyes
speak in a tongue
no book has ever written,
no land has ever claimed.

A foreign language—
born of glances and pauses,
of storms hidden behind calm seas.

And yet,
every syllable
falls into my heart like it belongs there,
as if I've been fluent
all my life.

15. Unmourned

The idea of
Dying alone doesn't feel that bad now
My corpse laying
And nobody's crying

The silence whispers
No footsteps near
A fading presence
In the absence of fear

No need for sorrow
No last goodbye
Just peaceful darkness
Beneath the sky.

16. Silent Sobs of Night

In the stillness of the night
When darkness veils the sky
A gentle rain of tears descends,
A sorrows multiply.
The weight upon my weary heart,
A burden hard to bear,
I seek solace in the darkness,
Finding refugee there

As moonlight softly dances,
Casting on the wall
My tears become a symphony,
A melody that call.
Each drop that falls upon my cheek,
A release from deep within.
Cleaning wounds and healing scars,
Like a soothing violin.

The night becomes my canvas, where emotions freely
flow.
Painting shades of sadness, with every tear that
I let go.

17. Where No Flags Fly

I live in places between
 Where no laws look,
Where no names are asked.

Am I a traitor?
Or a soldier in a war, no one sees?

I live between borders
Not countries,
but places where eyes don't follow
and silence is safe.

A world of walls,
Another world of fire,
And we meet at ashes.

People ask to be seen in daylight.
 But mine wears boots,
Carries map of place I cannot stay.

They built a world for clean love
But what I found burns through paper.
No anthems sings for it; No God claims it.
Still, it breathes.

Even rebels need a place to ache.
To write history, that no one will ever read.

Some things are more dangerous,
When you give them names.

People will say I am lost.
They will say I betrayed something sacred.

Let them keep their tidy stories.
Let them sit safe inside their lines.

And let me bled quietly.

So we meet in the smoke,
Between what is allowed,
And what is alive

Because not all resistance wears a gun
Some wears a smile.

And we
stay there.
Unforgiven.
Unlabeled.
Unmoving.

18. Whispering Wind

This sleepless night is dedicated to you.

How are you?
I asked, but what I really want
Is to feel your presence near
To hold my hand and soothe my fear.

A light hug, reassuring words
Tell me I'll be alright, I know it hurts
I just want you to be proud of me
For all strength I try to show,
For Her...
...for Us.

But in the end, it all comes crashing down.
And I left alone, pretending to be strong
Raw emotions flow, tears fell like rain
My heart's pain...is plain

in the end it hurts.

19. Land of Ghost

When I'm gone forever,
Far away in the land of ghost,
Where no one can ever hold me close.

Don't grieve for me
Just cremate me in serene.

But in spring just gather some flowers
And remember the place I lay.

20. Eternal Muse

Things are going wrong again,
and I wonder
till when
will my grief be my muse?

My heart clenches tight,
yet the pain feels strangely sweet.
Glossy eyes blur the world,
a throat pressed shut
by words unsaid.

A hollow ache settles in my chest,
and drifts downward, heavy,
until it twists in the stomach...
a reminder I cannot escape.

This kind of pain always finds me,
For it is my muse for eternity.

21. Smell of Freedom

In the open air, I breathe
I Soar
Freedom's scent, forever more
Boundless joy
With new found wings
I now abide

In every step, a liberation song
No chains of doubt, no ties, no wrong.

I found my peace,
The fragrance of freedom,
Sweet and clear.

www.ingramcontent.com/pod-product-compliance
Lightning Source LLC
Chambersburg PA
CBHW051001030426
42339CB00007B/434

Red with Memories is a collection of poems about love, loss, and the thoughts that keep you awake at night.
It speaks of quiet pain, fragile hope, and the beauty of feeling deeply — even when it hurts.
Each poem is a piece of healing, a whisper from the heart that refused to stay silent.

ABOUT THE AUTHOR

Rodali Kalita is a college student pursuing an undergraduate degree in Botany at Bhattadev University.
She writes poetry drawn from love, loss, and late-night thoughts — capturing emotions that often go unspoken.
Red with Memories is her debut collection, a heartfelt reflection on what it means to feel, break, and heal.

BookLeaf
Publishing
India | USA | UK

LAYERS

D'Shan Berry